LASELL COLLEGE
3 3015 00109 0629

W9-AFG-372

LET'S INVESTIGATE ART

# STORIES IN ART

Clare Gogerty

Artwork by Lis Watkins

Marshall Cavendish
New York • London • Toronto • Sydney

Published by
**Marshall Cavendish Corporation**
2415 Jerusalem Avenue
P.O. Box 587
North Bellmore, New York 11710



Designed and produced by Touchstone Publishing Ltd



Designer: David Armitage
Editor: Edwina Conner

Cover: *Rustam Killing the White Demon,* from a mid-seventeenth-century Persian book, the *Shah Nemeh*

Picture acknowledgements: see page 47

**Library of Congress Cataloging-in-Publication Data**

Gogerty, Clare.
Stories in art / Clare Gogerty : artwork, Lis Watkins.
p. cm. — (Let's investigate art)
Includes index.
ISBN 1-85435-767-O (set). — ISBN 1-85435-770-O (vol.)
1. Art—Themes, motives—Juvenile literature. 2. Art appreciation—Juvenile literature. [1. Art appreciation.] I. Watkins, Lis, ill. II. Title. III. Series: Gogerty, Clare. Let's investigate art.
N7560.G65 1994 94-8957
701'.1—dc20 CIP
AC

Printed in Italy
Bound in the USA

# Contents


**1** History in pictures 4
**2** Gods and heroes 10
**3** Fabulous beasts 16
**4** Religious stories 22
**5** Everyday life 28
**6** Stories in print 34
**7** Moving pictures 40

About the artists 46
Acknowledgements 47
Index 48


In every chapter of this book you will find a number of colored boxes. Each one has a symbol at the top to tell you what type of box it is:

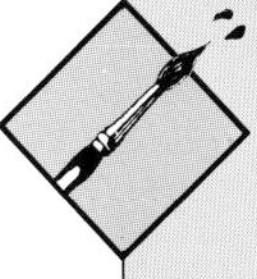

**Activity box.** Ideas for projects that will give you an insight into the techniques of the artists in this book. Try your hand at painting, sculpting, and crafts.

**Information box.** Detailed explanations of particular aspects of the text, or in-depth information on an artist or work of art.

**Look and See box.** Suggestions for some close observation, using this book, the library, art galleries, and the art and architecture in your area.

# History in pictures

This morning you may have heard the news on the radio or read the headlines in the newspaper. Or perhaps you watched the news on television last night? Living in the fast-moving twentieth century, we are used to learning about events all over the world almost as soon as they happen. But think what it was like in the days before printing was invented, when the fastest way of conveying information was by horse and rider, and news had to be written by hand or spoken aloud. People sometimes had to wait months to hear news of wars going on in their own country, let alone abroad. In those times, pictures could tell people about important events.

## *History in the making*

When the Normans invaded Britain in 1066, they fought a great battle at Hastings. The English king, Harold, was killed, shot through the eye with an arrow. One way we know about this event is from a piece of needlework that told the story in pictures. It is called the Bayeux Tapestry.

In the Middle Ages, many people lived in castles with thick, cold walls. Rich people

▼ *This is a scene from the Bayeux Tapestry, which is the length of about five football fields! William the Conqueror and his troops are charging into battle against King Harold and the English army. Originally the colors were much brighter, but they have faded with time. The strange-looking animals in the borders are for decoration. How have the embroiderers represented the soldiers' armor?*

### A stitch in time

Despite its name, the Bayeux Tapestry is not really a tapestry at all but an embroidery. A tapestry is woven on a loom, but the Bayeux Tapestry was sewn with needles and brightly colored wool by a group of women. They carefully stitched the action of the battle following the artist's design. Experts think it was sewn by English women, not French women, even though the story of the Battle of Hastings is told from the French point of view.

Works of art using needle, thread, and material were often produced by women, though these days men are often as skilled in needlecraft as women are. For a long time, women had to make all the clothes for the family, and the household sewing box contained plenty of materials useful for more creative work.

In America, women took pride in quilt-making, which is still popular today. These quilts are made of many pieces of fabric sewn together and then embroidered. They often include scenes from a family's history or other historical or political events.

employed needlewomen to weave tapestries or embroider linen with brightly colored wool to make hangings to cover the walls. They must have brought a feeling of warmth and color to the bleak castle rooms.

Most of the wall hangings were purely decorative. But some depicted the adventures of heroes and told stories of saints. Many castles were destroyed or ransacked, and the tapestries were lost forever. The Bayeux tapestry survived because it was kept in a cathedral.

## *Words and pictures*

News reached people more quickly once printing was invented, but pictures were still important. Rich and powerful people still wanted a record of themselves and their deeds. Religious authorities still wanted people to learn about their religion. Even when books were available, many people could not read. Now, as then, a picture often tells a story better and quicker than words can. Pictures are still hung in public places to remind people of some great event in the nation's history or tell the story of a famous person.

## *Official artists*

Sometimes governments or other authorities pay artists to record events of national importance as they happen. They ask, or commission, "official artists" to do the job. Even though we now have photography to record every grim detail of a war, official war artists still accompany troops to the front line to paint what they see there. An artist can create an atmosphere of fear, horror, triumph, or happiness more easily than a photographer.

The artist Jacques Louis David was the official artist of the French Revolution (1789-1799). David was a supporter of the revolutionaries. His portraits of the leaders, and of Napoleon who took over from them, make them look valiant and grand. He painted them as he would have liked them to be. His pictures stirred the hearts of French people who were proud of their country.

From 1939-1945, artists created paintings of World War II, and in the late 1980s, the Imperial War Museum in London commissioned artist John Keane to illustrate the events of the Gulf War.

▲ *Jean-Paul Marat was a supporter of the French Revolution. Because of a painful skin condition, he sat in a bath much of the day. One day, a woman named Charlotte Corday came to see him with a petition to sign. As he read it, she stabbed him to death. Why do you think the artist did not include the murderer in the picture?*
[The Death of Marat, *Jacques Louis David*]

## *Propaganda*

Governments try to persuade people to accept their point of view. They may do this by using propaganda – leaflets, television programs, posters, news briefings – that show them in a good light. Artistic images make excellent propaganda, because they provide a simple picture-story of a situation, whether it is true or not.

The government of the former Soviet Union, for example, wanted people to think that it was doing a good job and that they were living in wonderful times. It wanted people to work harder and

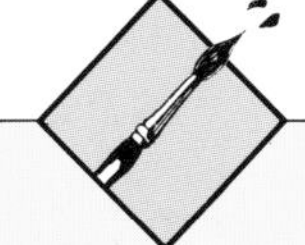

Design a poster for an issue that concerns you, your class at school, or your community. Make it a strong image and try to get your poster to tell a story.

▶ *The slave trade was abolished in the United States in 1807. Before that, thousands of people were brought from West Africa by traders who sold them to households and plantations. It was a terrible life and many slaves tried to escape. In this picture the owners' dogs have hunted down two runaway slaves. Notice the man's broken handcuffs. How has the artist created a sense of fear and desperation?* [Hunted Slaves, *Richard Ansdell*]

not complain. It asked artists to design posters that would put these messages across. They came up with strong, heroic pictures that would, they hoped, inspire all those who saw them.

## *Degenerate art*

Some art does not meet with a government's approval. Adolf Hitler, the leader of Nazi Germany in the 1930s and 1940s, insisted that only art he approved of could be exhibited. Like the rulers of the Soviet Union, he wanted the German people to believe in positive, flattering images of himself and his party. He wanted them to see a version of Germany that he had created. Art that did not fit in with Hitler's ideas was called degenerate art and was banned. Degenerate means corrupt and low, but the work in question was generally neither; it was simply truthful. Many artists fled the country so that they could paint what they wanted, not what Hitler dictated. The artists that Hitler admired are long forgotten, while the so-called degenerates, including Marc Chagall and Otto Dix, are highly regarded now in Germany and all over the world. In Germany and other democratic countries today, artists are free to paint exactly what they like.

## *Stories on the wall*

Some governments and official bodies commission pictures to decorate the walls inside and outside public buildings. Big businesses

A narrative is another name for a story. Pictures that tell stories are called narrative paintings. Whenever you see a picture with people in it, figure out what it is about before you read or find out about it. Look at the pictures in this book before you read the captions. Figure out what story each picture is telling.

sometimes commission wall paintings for their offices. Pictures painted on walls (rather than in frames) are called murals. Because they are painted in public places, many people can see murals.

In 1920, the Mexican artist Diego Rivera visited Italy. He saw for the first time murals painted hundreds of years before by artists of the Italian Renaissance (see page 25). The paintings, which decorated the walls of churches and cathedrals, were all religious. The artists used the technique called fresco-painting (see above).

Back in Mexico, Rivera painted frescoes of his own. Their object was not religious, but political. In exuberant colors, he told the story of his

### On the wall

A fresco is a type of wall painting where, instead of painting on canvas or board, the artist paints on wet plaster. First the design is drawn on fresh plaster with charcoal (charred wood). The design is then cut into the surface. Then a fine layer of plaster is applied in small sections over the rough plaster so the design still shows through. Finally the artist paints the picture on the new, wet plaster.

▼ *This fresco by Diego Rivera explains how the Spanish invasion and conquest of Mexico in 1519 led to terrible hardship and slavery.* [The Spanish Conquest, *Diego Rivera*]

*► For many years, the German city of Berlin was divided by a high wall. People hated the wall and painted pictures on it to express their feelings.*

country in the 400 years before the Mexican Revolution of 1915, when Mexico was ruled by Spain. Paid for by the government of Mexico, his brilliant pictures decorate the walls of many public buildings. The people can enjoy the colorful scenes and get a picture of their country's history.

## *Murals around you*

In the present, local authorities might commission murals to brighten up a neighbourhood and make it cheerful for everyone living there. They generally like the subject to be of public interest, so murals often show important local events or the lives of famous people. They hope that, if the place looks attractive, people will take pride in it and keep it pleasant. They hope to discourage people from scrawling graffiti or spraying paint on the walls and spoiling the environment for everyone.

### Pictures in plaster

You may not be able to plaster a wall and paint it, but you can very easily make a block of plaster of Paris, plaster filler, or molding clay and paint a design on it.

**What you need**

- large plastic tray or shallow container with sides
- bag of plaster of Paris, plaster filler, or molding plaster
- large jug of water
- watercolors
- sand

**What you do**

1. Mix the plaster of Paris by adding the powder to the water (about 1½ times more powder than water).

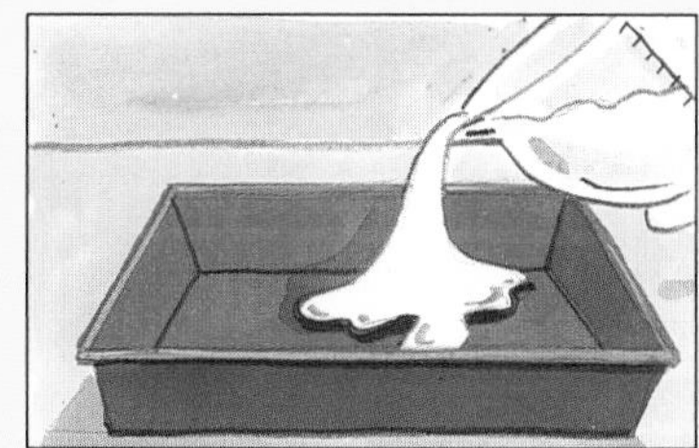

2. Pour the plaster into the tray and wait for it to set.

3. Remove the plaster from the mold and paint your picture in bright colors while the plaster is still wet.

# Gods and heroes

Every nation has its own myths and legends. These are strange, often magical stories that are handed down through the centuries and become part of a country's culture. The main characters in the stories are often gods and goddesses or heroes and heroines with special qualities and powers. Although the characters in each country's stories are different, the plots are often similar. They are tales of bravery, love, revenge, and intrigue that have inspired artists for thousands of years.

## Greek myths

Some Greek myths try to explain how the world began. These stories are called "creation myths." The gods and goddesses of ancient Greek mythology often appear in stories involving human beings. They often befriended mortal men and women and protected them from the anger of other gods as they went about their adventures.

◀ *Greek mythology tells of a race of fierce warrior women called the Amazons. They were trained to fight and hunt when they were little girls. In this stone frieze (which was carved in 350 B.C.), an Amazon is shown attacking a Greek soldier. Who do you think is winning? How can you tell? Notice the way the Amazon's clothes emphasize the movement of her body.*

### Greek gods and goddesses

According to legend, Greek gods and goddesses made their home on Mount Olympus, the highest peak in Greece. Each one had a particular role to play. Here are ten of them. Try to find pictures of these and other deities.

**Zeus** – protector and ruler of all the gods and son of Cronos. He won the universe from Cronos and shared it with his brothers.

**Poseidon** – brother of Zeus and god of the sea.

**Hades** – another brother of Zeus, and ruler of the underworld.

**Hera** – one of Zeus's wives, often unhappy and cruel.

**Apollo** – the Greek god of medicine, music, and prophecy. As an infant, he was fed on nectar and ambrosia (special foods for the gods), which helped him grow to manhood in just four days.

**Demeter** – sister of Zeus and goddess of the fruitful earth. Her daughter was carried off by Hades to be his queen and she is often shown as a sorrowing mother.

**Triton** – son of Poseidon, often portrayed as a merman, human above the waist and fish below.

**Aphrodite** – goddess of love, beauty, and fertility.

**Athene** – daughter of Zeus and his first wife, Metis. Zeus swallowed Metis when she was pregnant, in case she bore a son who would overthrow him. Athene was born when she emerged, fully armed, from Zeus's head.

**Pan** – a herdsman's god, often depicted as part goat. He was a good musician and played the pan pipes, as shepherds in parts of Greece still do today.

Ancient Greek characters pit their wits and strength against the supernatural powers of the gods. You can see why these stories have been so popular with artists: they are just as exciting as modern comics featuring superheroes.

The ancient Greeks worshipped and prayed in temples dedicated to particular gods and goddesses. Sometimes they brought offerings or made sacrifices in front of the statue of a god. These statues were superb works of art created by talented sculptors who had to make the statues look god-like. To do this they made the figures ideal human beings. Their bodies are in perfect proportion and their faces have no marks or deformities. Some ancient Greeks thought that the gods themselves lived inside these statues.

Unfortunately, not much sculpture from this time exists today. Much was destroyed by Christian and other invaders who disapproved of "pagan idols" and found the massive stones of ancient monuments useful for building castles. Fortunately, some copies of the statues were made. Most of these are solemn figures made of white marble. Originally, however, many of the statues were painted in lifelike colors. Some were made of wood and decorated with gold, ivory, and precious stones. Others were made of bronze, but were melted down later when bronze became scarce.

## Make a Greek theater

Find a Greek myth that interests you and make a scene of a dramatic event in it, using a cardboard box and cut-out figures.

This scene tells the story of Perseus and Medusa. Medusa was a beautiful young girl who annoyed the goddess Minerva. To punish her, Minerva turned Medusa's hair into snakes and made her so frightening that anyone who looked at her was turned to stone. The Greek hero Perseus went to her cave and managed to cut off her head with his sword by looking at her reflection in his shield rather than by looking at her face. In this way he escaped being turned to stone.

### What you do

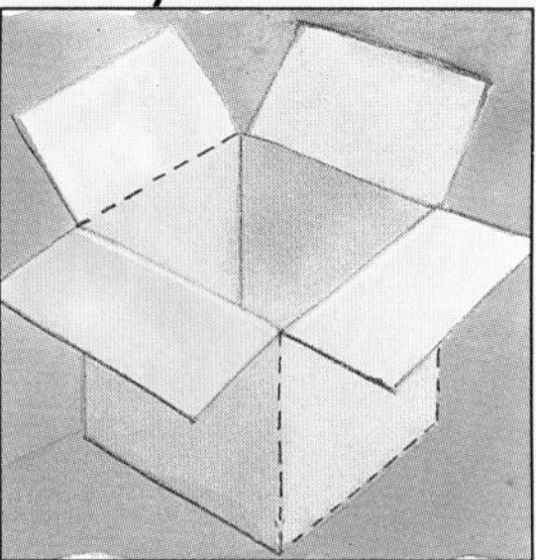

1. Take an ordinary cardboard grocery box, with flaps on top.

2. Turn it sideways so the flaps open sideways, and cut off the "top"; this will be the backdrop. Paint this and the front flaps of your box. This is your scenery.

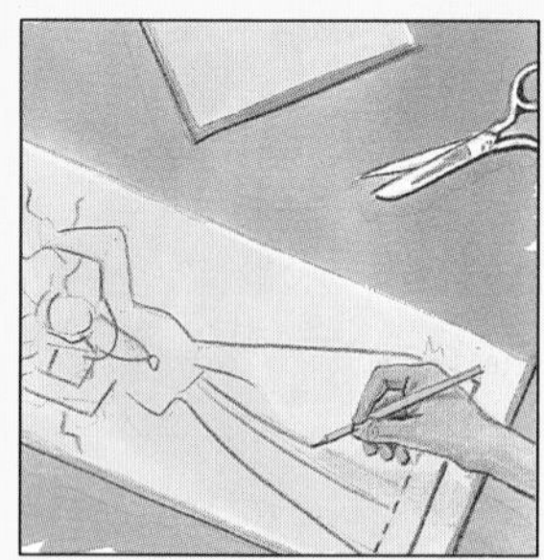

3. Draw your figures on some cardboard, leaving a flap at the bottom to turn under so that the figures stand up. Paint the figures and cut them out.

4. Make more figures for other scenes so that you can show all the events in your story.

As well as free-standing statues, sculptors also carved beautiful stone friezes that tell picture stories of these ancient gods and goddesses.

## *Living legends*

Unlike myths, legends are at least partly true and are about real people, not gods or goddesses. Nevertheless, they

▲ *The knights in the English legend of King Arthur spent much of their time searching for the Holy Grail (a chalice, or cup, used by Jesus). In this tapestry, one knight, Sir Galahad, finds it. He was the noblest of all the knights, and is shown surrounded by lilies, which are often used in art as symbols of purity. The three figures on the left are angels. Why do you think they are there?* [Quest for the Holy Grail, *tapestry from a design by Sir Edward Burne-Jones*]

often tell of magic and the supernatural. Because legends were not written down, they were passed by word of mouth down the centuries.

Many British artists of the Victorian period, such as Edward Burne-Jones, Dante Gabriel Rossetti, George Watts, and Lord Leighton, painted legends. Britain at this time was in the middle of the Industrial Revolution. New factories had been built and towns were filled with smoke from their chimneys. The population had grown and poorer people lived crowded together in inadequate housing. Many people were very poor and health care was not good.

Instead of painting the gray and depressing world around them, these Victorian artists depicted another romantic world based on the legends of the past, filled with beauty and color. Edward Burne-Jones was brought up near the industrial slums. He described what he painted as "a beautiful romantic dream of something that never was, in a land no one can remember, only desire."

Burne-Jones chose Greek myths and other legends as subjects for his paintings. He liked the way that these stories emphasized the beauty of nature and were filled with mystery and melancholy. He particularly liked the legends of King Arthur and the Knights of the Round Table, which tell of heroism, chivalry, love, and magic.

If you look at a picture from Japan and one from Persia (modern-day Iran) – there's one of each in this chapter – you can see immediately how different the style of painting is. Almost every culture has produced a distinctive type of painting. Look at pictures in this book, and elsewhere, and see if you can tell which country they come from.

## *Stories around the world*

Japan is a country rich in folklore and legends. The old legends are kept alive today in art, books, the theater, and the cinema. Many of the stories are about the supernatural. Artists such as Hokusai drew illustrations for books that

▼ *This woodblock print tells of a famous Japanese legend. A noble was made to kill himself because he had wounded an important official. To avenge his death, forty-seven of the noble's samurai, or warriors, attacked the official's castle and killed him. Their costumes are decorated with black and white triangles. How many samurai can you see? What season is it?* [Scene from the Kabuki play Chushingura, *Utagawa Kuniyoshi*]

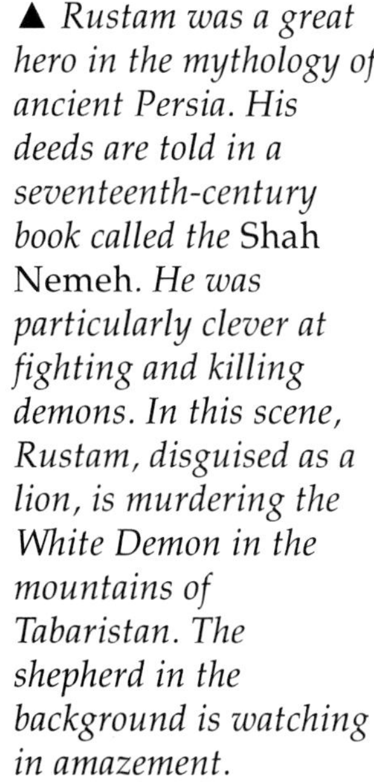

▲ *Rustam was a great hero in the mythology of ancient Persia. His deeds are told in a seventeenth-century book called the* Shah Nemeh. *He was particularly clever at fighting and killing demons. In this scene, Rustam, disguised as a lion, is murdering the White Demon in the mountains of Tabaristan. The shepherd in the background is watching in amazement.*

told these stories. The pictures were printed in the books, not hung on walls. Hokusai drew brave warriors, eerie ghosts, and frightened maidens who were rescued from villains.

In the nineteenth century, the bright colors and unusual designs of Japanese prints influenced Western artists, such as Edgar Degas and Vincent Van Gogh, who used many of the ideas in their own work.

## Woodblock prints

The Japanese picture by Kuniyoshi in this chapter was produced by a method known as woodblock printing. Woodblock printing was once very popular in Japan. Prints were produced entirely by hand. Teams of craftsmen worked together in a workshop to make prints. Their boss was a man called a publisher who was in charge of the workshop.

First of all, the artist would provide a sketch, which he drew in black ink on white paper. He gave this to the publisher, who asked another craftsman to copy the design onto thin paper. This was given to an engraver, who pasted it on a block of seasoned cherry wood.

Then all the parts of the picture that were one color – red, say – were carved with knives and tools called gouges, leaving only the raised lines of the image to be printed. The block was coated with ink, and a piece of paper laid on top of it. Then the back of the paper was rubbed with a soft pad so the ink was transferred onto it. A new block was used for each color, and the picture was built up layer by layer. The printer had to position the paper carefully for each color. Finally, the finished print was hung up to dry. Because it was possible to make many prints from one block, they were pasted into books or sold singly in large numbers in markets all over Japan.

# Fabulous beasts

As well as gods and heroes, all sorts of weird and wonderful animals appear in myths and legends. The ancient Greeks told stories about many strange creatures, some of which were half human, half beast. A satyr was half goat, half man. A centaur had the head, arms, and torso of a man, but the legs of a horse. The Minotaur was a fierce creature that had the body of a man and the head of a bull. It lived in a labyrinth (an underground maze) and fed on human flesh – until it was killed by the hero Theseus.

▼ *In Greek myths, Sirens were fabulous creatures with the bodies of birds and the heads of women. They would lure men to their deaths by singing sweetly to them. This vase painting shows the hero Odysseus, who has been tied to the mast of a ship so that he doesn't fall into the Sirens' deadly trap and steer his ship on to the rocks. Notice how the artist has made the picture fit the shape of the vase.*

## Greek vase painting

In ancient Greece, vases were not used for holding flowers as they are today, but for storing oil and wine. Others were made to go inside tombs. They were decorated with pictures of the dead person surrounded by mourners and objects that the deceased owned during his or her lifetime. Every one had to be made and decorated by hand because there were no machines to do the job. The artists who decorated the vases were highly skilled and very famous at the time. Many of them lived in the city of Athens, where making and decorating vases was an important industry. As you look carefully at a Greek vase, a story – usually from a myth – unfolds. In a tiny space, the artist uses clear outlines, with little shading or pattern, to make heroes and monsters spring into life and create a story.

▼ *Dragons appear in stories and pictures all over the world. Although they vary in size and shape, they all have scaly bodies and fire-breathing nostrils. In China, huge models of dragons are carried through the streets on special days, such as Chinese New Year. They twist and turn as though they are alive. The Chinese people believe the dragons will frighten away evil spirits and make room for good spirits.*

## *Monsters with a message*

Throughout history, people have claimed the existence of imaginary beasts, such as the unicorn with its single, magical horn, or dragons that breathed fire, or in our own day, a prehistoric monster that lives in a Scottish lake – the Loch Ness monster.

During the Middle Ages in Europe, woodcarvers and stonemasons decorated churches with all kinds of monsters. They carved the creatures in wood or stone – devils with horns, snakes swallowing their own tails, the creatures of the zodiac, and all manner of strange beasts conjured up by the imagination.

These carvings had a purpose. They reminded people of what would happen to them after death if they led wicked lives. They would go to hell and be tormented by fiends and demons like those they saw around them. If they led good lives, however, they would go to heaven and live with the saints whose images were also carved inside and outside the churches.

If you look high up on a medieval church, you will see grotesque monsters just below the roof. As well as keeping the faithful fearful, they also kept the roof dry. The beasts were hollowed out to let the rain run off the roof and down through their bodies.

## *Dragons for good and evil*

Although there are plenty of odd-looking lizards and other reptiles, winged, fire-eating dragons have never existed outside stories. In western culture, dragons are wicked creatures that threaten humans and can only be defeated by heroes. The most famous dragon slayer was St. George. He killed a dragon to save a young maiden.

In the east, dragons are more friendly. The people of China believe that dragons have the power to banish evil. Every year, Chinese people all over the world celebrate their New Year with festivals and parties. They parade huge paper dragons through the streets. These dragons scare

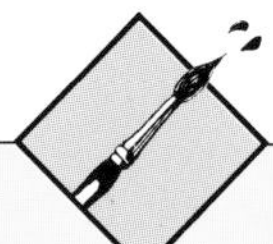

## Your own fabulous beast

Look at the pictures of fabulous beasts in this chapter and at dinosaurs and other monsters in books. Children's books are full of them. Make some charcoal drawings of whichever creatures capture your imagination, and make up some of your own.

### What you need

- large piece of paper. Use the back of a spare piece of wallpaper or a piece of paper used to line drawers or shelves
- charcoal
- pencil
- charcoal fixer
- red marker

### What you do

1. Using a pencil, sketch the outline of your beasts very lightly and loosely.
2. Draw over the pencil marks in charcoal. Add more charcoal lines to give it more form. Make good, bold lines. Rub over parts of your drawing with a finger to smudge it a little. Charcoal makes dark marks and light ones. Use both kinds in your drawing. Try and leave some areas white so that they contrast with the dark charcoal.
3. Give your monsters red eyes!
4. If you want to keep your picture, spray it with charcoal fixer, which you can buy in art shops. This will keep the charcoal from smudging.

▲ *At first this carving looks like a complicated pattern of leaves and branches. But if you look closely you will see a man killing a dragon. The man is Sigurd, a hero from Viking legends, who was the son of the god Odin. The dragon, which had the body of a snake, is called Fafnir. See how the figures are tangled up in the vegetation. Do you think this makes the scene more exciting or less?*

away the bad things so that the new year will be a good one. Dragons have always been popular in Chinese art. In the thirteenth century, Chinese artists painted dragons on long strips of paper called scrolls. They rolled up the scrolls and kept them safe in containers. Their owners unrolled them occasionally and hung them up for family and friends to admire and enjoy.

## *Beasts from the north*

The Vikings were a fearsome race. They sailed from the north (Norse) countries of Europe and invaded other countries, looting and pillaging and devastating the countryside.

But they did not only fight. They were fine craftsmen, skilled artists, and excellent storytellers. They loved complicated patterns and often included the twisted bodies of dragons and serpents in their designs. These creatures appear in their legends and were also used to decorate their ships. The god Odin rode an eight-legged stallion called Sleipnir and did battle with a giant wolf called Fenrir. The thunder god Thor fought in vain against a great sea monster called the serpent of Midgard. Like Poseidon, the Greek god of the sea, this legendary creature caused the storms that the seafaring Vikings so dreaded.

## *Totem poles*

Some native peoples in North America and in the Pacific islands recorded their stories on tall wooden poles – tree trunks that had been stripped and smoothed. They carved strange animals and masks. Each carving on the pole represents a scene from a legend. You "read" the story from the bottom upward. The images on the poles are starkly simple. For example, a bird may be shown as a mask with a beak and nothing else. There is little movement in the figures and they do not relate to one another, but they are so expressive that the story can be understood.

Each totem pole tells the stories of the tribe that made it. The poles were objects of reverence, so the carvers took immense care and pride in their construction. All the men in the tribe helped with the carving and painting, which took years to complete.

Learn more about the original inhabitants of North America. What kind of art did they produce? What animals did they depict? How have Native American art and culture influenced North America today?

### Tribal art

Totem poles are an example of what some call primitive art. This term was thought up at the beginning of the twentieth century by explorers who came into contact with people in countries far away from their own. They were living in ways that had changed little in centuries. The lives of these people had been unaffected by the scientific and technological advances of the western world. Today, fewer peoples follow traditional ways of life, but their art continues to tell their story.

The art of tribal people was seldom simply decorative. It had a purpose. Sculpture, masks, and carvings usually had a religious role, such as maintaining contact with the dead or with the gods. Many western artists, such as Picasso, have been greatly influenced by the beauty and simplicity of tribal art.

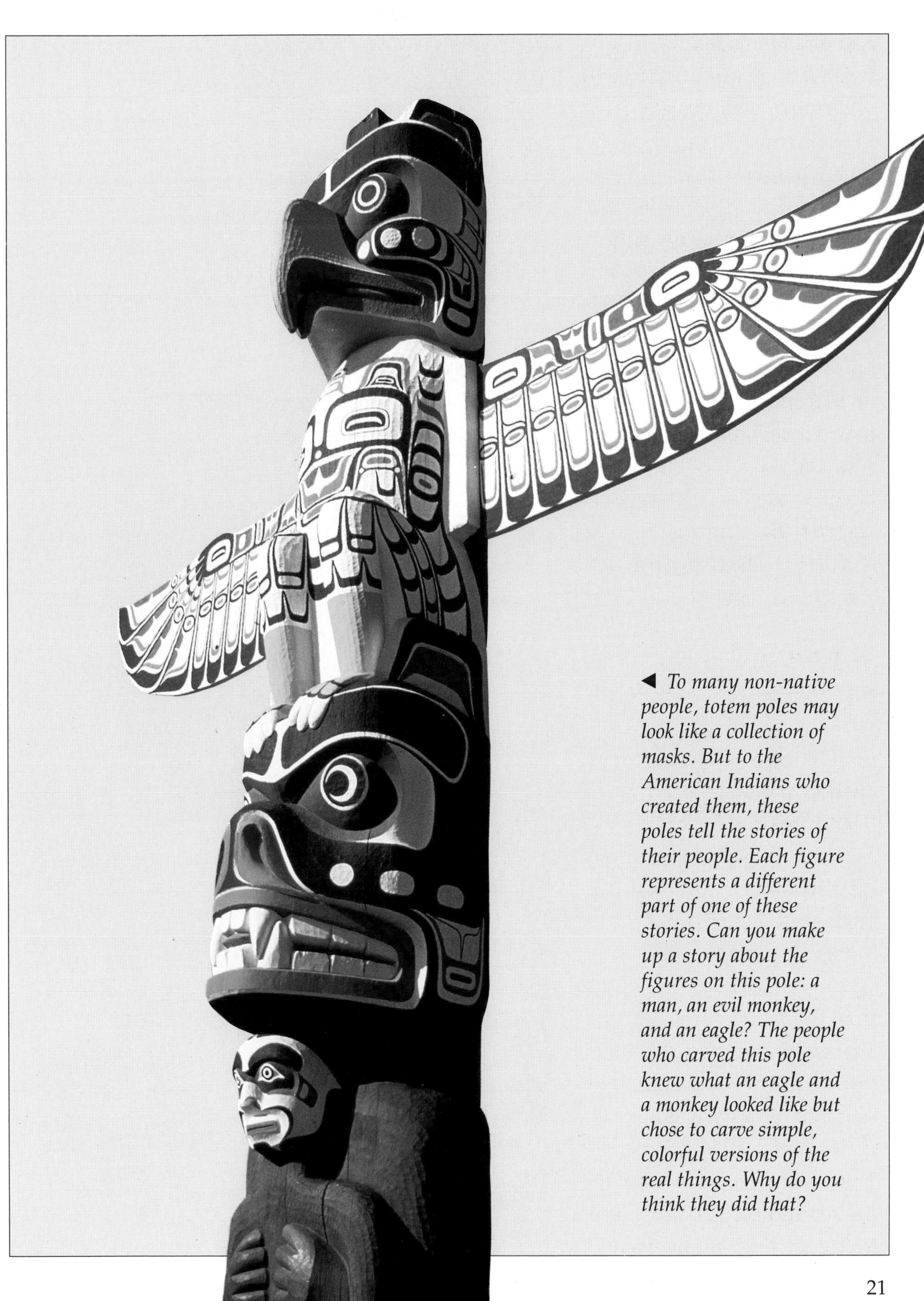

◀ *To many non-native people, totem poles may look like a collection of masks. But to the American Indians who created them, these poles tell the stories of their people. Each figure represents a different part of one of these stories. Can you make up a story about the figures on this pole: a man, an evil monkey, and an eagle? The people who carved this pole knew what an eagle and a monkey looked like but chose to carve simple, colorful versions of the real things. Why do you think they did that?*

# 4 Religious stories

The beliefs and teachings of every religion in the world are based on collections of stories. These stories are told in holy books: the Old Testament of the Bible (Jewish), the Old and New Testaments of the Bible (Christian), the Koran (Islamic), and the *Mahabharata* (Hindu).

Before people could read, religious pictures taught them about their faith. It was important to make people understand the teachings, so the paintings had to be simple and the stories told clearly. In many ways they were like the picture books that children read today.

▼ *The story of Job is in the Old Testament. He was tested by the devil, who made him suffer many hardships to see if he would keep his faith in God. This stained-glass window shows his herdsmen being killed by soldiers. Job never lost his faith and, as a reward, God made him richer than before.*

## Window dressing

The picture of Job's herdsmen (right) is made out of glass and pieces of lead. To make a stained-glass window like this, the artist first drew a design on a wooden panel. Then he or his helpers cut the glass to match the shapes he had drawn. On the glass he painted details such as faces, hands, and folds in people's clothes with brown pigment. Then the craftsmen fired the pieces of glass in a kiln, joined them together with strips of lead, and set the completed window in an iron frame. At first, stained-glass craftsmen only had blue and red glass. Later, other colors became available. Now a full range of colors can be manufactured. If a stained-glass window is mostly red and blue, it probably dates back to the twelfth century.

## Make a "stained glass" panel

Although it is too difficult and too expensive to make a real stained glass window, you can make an effective copy from cardboard and tissue paper.

### What you need

- colored tissue paper or colored cellophane
- scissors
- pencil
- black cardboard (8 1/2 x 11 inches)
- glue
- double-sided tape

### What you do

1. Take the rectangular piece of black cardboard and fold it in half.
2. Sketch a simple design onto the cardboard, such as the sun shown here. Keep the shapes simple to make the cutting out easy.
3. Cut the design through both sheets of the cardboard with a sharp knife or scissors. You may need an adult's help.
4. Cut out pieces of tissue paper or cellophane, using your black cutouts as a guide. Allow a little extra all around each shape so that you can glue them on.
5. On the back of one of the pieces of cardboard, dab glue around the edges of the holes that you cut out. Stick the pieces of cellophane or tissue over the matching holes.
6. Glue the other piece of cardboard to the back of your first piece, so you have a sandwich with the tissue paper or cellophane in the middle.
7. Press together firmly and leave under a heavy book to dry.
8. Stick your "stained-glass" panel onto a window with a piece of double-sided tape and watch the sun shine through.

## *Rules for the artist*

There were often strict rules for artists to follow when painting religious pictures. Islam forbids artists to paint figures in a religious place. As a result, Islamic mosques are covered in mosaics and other decoration of semi-abstract patterns. These designs are based on plants, flowers, and geometric shapes.

The art of beautiful handwriting is called calligraphy. In Islam, the important sayings of the prophet Mohammed are painted on the walls of the mosques for people to read. Calligraphy was important for Christians, too. Before printing was invented, monks handwrote the holy scriptures in a highly decorative style.

Although you never see religious figures decorating mosques, Muslim artists were allowed to include figures in

▼ *Although this painting shows a religious scene of the newborn baby Jesus with his mother, the figures look like ordinary people. Jesus looks like any other baby, and Mary is wearing simple clothes. Yet the painting still feels special and holy, because of the unusual light that seems to shine out from Jesus himself.* [The New Born Child, *Georges de La Tour*]

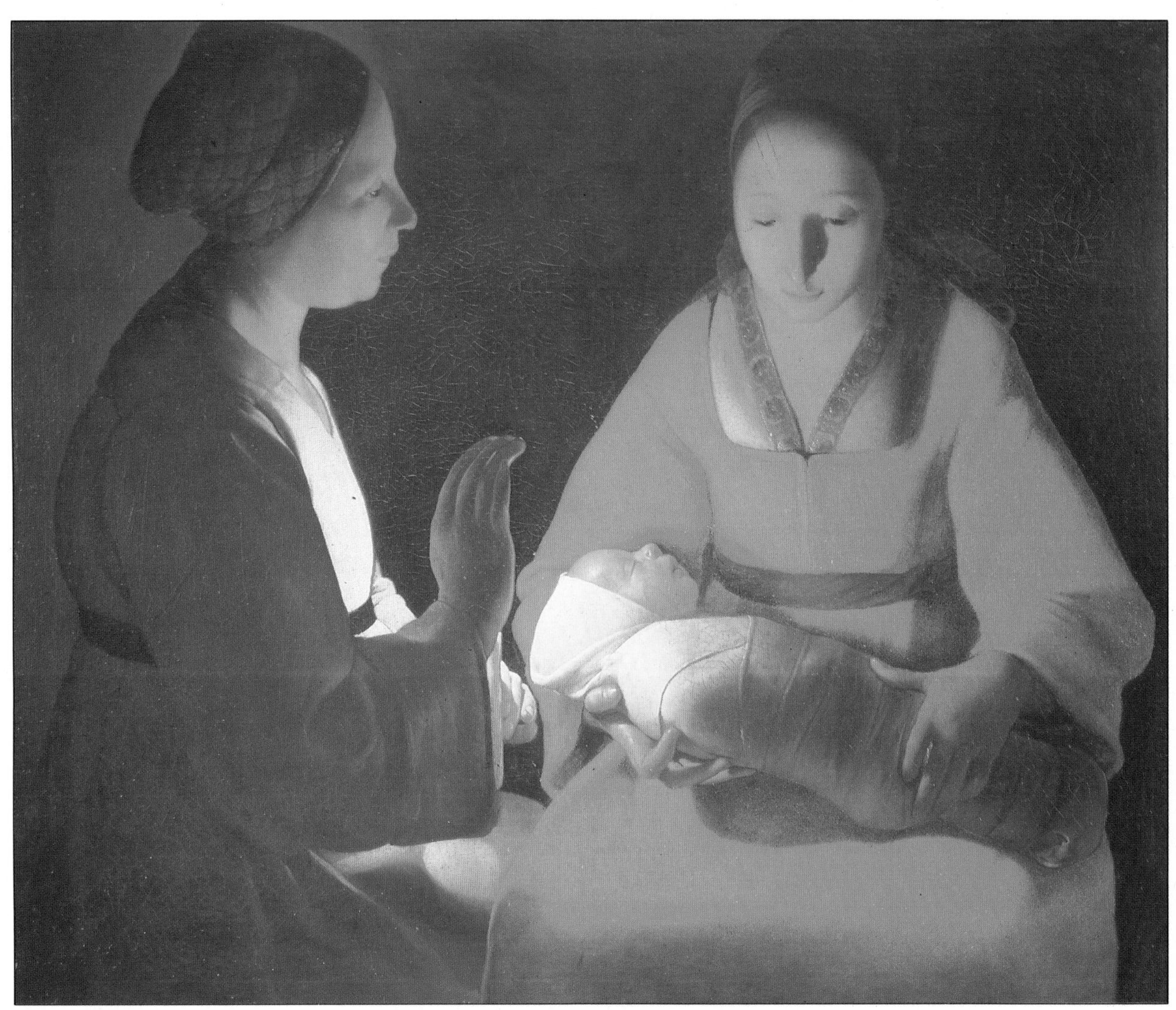

## The Renaissance

The Renaissance (a French word meaning "rebirth") is the name given to the period between about 1350 and 1550 in Italy. It was a time for introducing new ideas and rethinking old ones. Many of the new ideas in art and architecture were inspired by the works of the ancient Greeks and Romans, who made their art as beautiful and lifelike as possible. Before the Renaissance, artists painted figures in a stiff, formal manner and seemed to line them up along the edge of the picture frame.

Artists such as Giotto, Masaccio, and Mantegna painted people who looked as if they were made of real flesh and bone. They achieved this by clever use of light and shade and by carefully painting the way clothes hang and fall around the body. They used more colors than before to include a wider range of tones and shades. For the first time, Jesus was depicted as an ordinary man. Often the only way to recognize him in a painting with other figures is to look for his halo.

You do not need to go to an art gallery to see religious art. Churches and cathedrals are full of pictures, stained-glass windows, mosaics, and frescoes. In libraries, museums, synagogues, and mosques, you will find books, manuscripts, and works of art from many different religions. You do not have to follow a particular religion to find its stories and art attractive. Look at works of art from different faiths and get to know the stories they illustrate. See how they differ. See what they have in common.

book illustrations. Many Islamic books contained finely painted, colorful, and detailed pictures to accompany the sacred words.

During the Middle Ages, Christian artists could not show Jesus looking too much like an ordinary person. The Church felt that he should look like a god because people would not believe in someone who looked and behaved like a human being. Saints and the Holy Family were usually depicted with halos around their heads so it was clear who they were.

During the period called the Renaissance, this all changed. Later, in the sixteenth century, in the paintings of Caravaggio and Georges de La Tour, Jesus was shown eating, working, and behaving like an ordinary man. He wore normal clothes and mixed with real people. Many of the people in his company were shown to be dirty and had bare feet. This would have been unthinkable in an earlier age, and many people still thought that the paintings were sinful.

In the early days of the Christian church, statues were also frowned upon. They reminded people of pagan idols, which are condemned in the Bible. This also changed during the Renaissance, and statues of the Holy Family were placed in churches.

▲ *Buddha is the name given to an Indian noble, Gautama Siddhartha, who, like St. Francis, gave up his life of riches to become a holy man. One day, when he was sitting beneath a tree, he had a religious experience or "enlightenment." What he learned that day became the basis of Buddhism. In this carving, Buddha is shown meditating. Around him are scenes from his life. In the top left he is shown as a child beside his mother, and in the centre at the top he is dying peacefully. Can you see an elephant in the sculpture? Buddha is sitting in a position known as the lotus position. Can you sit like this? Be careful not to hurt yourself.*

▲ *The Hindu god Vishnu visited earth ten times, each time as a different person. Once he came as Krishna, a mischievous herdsman. Krishna angered Indra, the god of thunder, who sent a storm to drown him and his friends. For shelter, Krishna raised Mount Govardhana into the air with one finger and kept it there for seven days and nights. Indra was amazed and forgave him.*
[Krishna supporting Mount Govardhana, *Ustad Sahibdin*]

## *Eastern inspiration*

The story of the Buddha, unlike that of Jesus, has been told mainly through sculpture. Eastern religions have always stressed the importance of meditation. One form of meditation involves sitting in front of an object for a long time and thinking about it in different ways. Statues of the Buddha and sculptures showing scenes from his life inspire his followers to have religious thoughts as they meditate.

Pictures illustrating scenes from the sacred book, the *Mahabharata*, teach Hindus about their religion. At the same time they encourage the reader to live a good, heroic life by copying the way in which the gods Vishnu and Krishna acted.

These days much religious art is designed to be spiritually uplifting rather than teach facts about religion. As most people can read, there is less need to tell the stories through pictures.

# Everyday life

For a long period in the western world, people thought that everyday life was not a fit subject for art. Painters were only supposed to paint religious subjects. Popes and important people paid artists to paint portraits of themselves and pictures of the saints (often together), but an artist could not sell a picture of everyday life. Pictures of everyday life are called genre paintings. Fortunately, there are plenty of them now.

## *Life and death in Egypt*

The first pictures of everyday life were painted several thousand years ago in Egypt. The ancient Egyptians believed that when a person died, he or she would return to the lands of the gods. To help the dead person get there, the body was embalmed and put in a stone coffin inside a tomb. The tombs of important people were hidden inside huge pyramids that took many years to build.

▼ *Sennedjem was an ancient Egyptian master craftsman who lived around 1300 B.C. This painting is on the wall of his tomb. It shows Sennedjem guiding the plow and his wife scattering seed. The symbols behind them are hieroglyphs, the ancient Egyptian writing. Notice the patterns on the trees, on the clothes of the figures, and on the oxen. To the Egyptians, decoration and pattern were an important part of a tomb painting.*

▲ *This picture comes from a "book of hours" (a type of calendar) painted in the sixteenth century. Books of hours contained illustrations of the twelve months of the year. What can you see happening? Note that the mountains and river are painted in paler colors than the foreground. What effect does this have?* [Book of Hours (July), *Simon Benninck*]

Visit a modern art gallery and see what subjects interest artists of today. See if you can find some old manuscripts. Compare European manuscripts and pictures with those from India and Persia (modern Iran). See what stories they tell. See how much everyday life creeps into them.

The walls of the tomb were covered with pictures of the dead person's life on earth, which he or she hoped to recreate in the afterlife. The tombs were undisturbed for centuries, so they were safe from damage by people and by the weather. As a result, many of the wall paintings are in excellent condition. They look almost as fresh as the day they were painted.

As well as pictures of gods and pharaohs (kings), there are pictures of ordinary people going about their daily tasks – farmers and fishermen, potters and priests, people at work and at play. The people were painted in a highly stylized, formal way, but so clearly that we can tell how they lived.

## *Life in the Middle Ages*

For a long time after this, only serious, religious, or political themes were shown in art, especially in the western world. Some artists in the Middle Ages did, however, sneak more amusing scenes into their work. Monks had the laborious job of copying sacred scriptures in perfect script and decorating, or illuminating, them with pictures. The pictures in these manuscripts normally showed scenes from the Bible to go with the words.

Around the edges of the text in the margins of the book, the monks painted intricate pictures of everyday life. These pictures are called marginalia and include scenes of people hunting, farming and fighting. It is as though the artists were tired of the solemn things they had to paint and wanted to have some fun. Illuminated manuscripts were very expensive to produce and only rich people or religious organizations could afford to own one. Today, you can see examples of the original illuminated manuscripts in many museums and galleries. You can also find pictures of them in books.

## *At home in Holland*

It was in seventeenth-century Holland that pictures of ordinary life became popular. Wealthy businessmen wanted graceful, not grand, pictures to hang in their homes. From artists such as Vermeer and de Hooch, they commissioned pictures of ordinary people

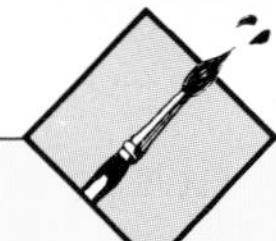

### Make an illuminated manuscript

Keep an illustrated diary that shows interesting events in your life. It does not have to be a daily diary, but something you take time over several times a year to make a record of your activities and achievements.

**What you need**

- scrapbook
- photos, tickets, other mementos
- photo mounts
- drawing materials
- glue
- pen

**What you do**

1. Whenever you enjoy a special treat, such as a meal out or a vacation, keep something to help you remember the occasion. The same applies to an important event such as a wedding, winning a sports award, the end of a school year, birth of a brother or sister.

2. Use your scrapbook to write down your thoughts and poems, paint pictures, and stick in photographs, tickets, and any other memorabilia you find in your pockets after the event.

3. Decorate the margins of your scrapbook carefully, as a monk would decorate an illuminated manuscript.

▼ *In the nineteenth century, African-Americans led hard lives, either as slaves or as poor freedmen. In the bottom right corner, a well-dressed white visitor peers into a world she knows nothing about. What do you think she is feeling and thinking? Was the artist sympathetic to the black people's situation?* [Old Kentucky Home Life in the South, *Eastman J. Johnson*]

doing ordinary things: a woman making lace, for example, or pouring milk, or playing a musical instrument.

Gradually, more and more artists began to paint the world as it was rather than idealizing it. Instead of seeing homely subjects as ugly and uninteresting, art buyers saw them as worthwhile and beautiful. People grew to love the paintings of Jean Baptiste Siméon Chardin, a French artist who painted children playing games or saying grace before a meal, or maids at work in the kitchen.

## Stories of home

The trend continued. In nineteenth-century France, Berthe Morisot painted comfortable, domestic scenes, while Edgar Degas painted women in the bath or ironing. These artists made genre painting popular in France.

Mary Cassatt, an American artist, painted loving pictures of mothers tending their children. Winslow Homer painted joyful scenes of American rural life. In Britain, genre painting was popularized by Sir David Wilkie, who brought Dutch ideas to Britain. He painted ordinary cottage life in Scotland, and many artists followed his lead in their own locales.

## Snap happy

David Hockney's picture of his mother (below) is made up of many different photographs. He could have painted his mother's portrait, but he chose to use a camera instead. Many artists use photography to create pictures. Because it is so quick to take, a photograph can capture an interesting image, especially outdoors, before it changes.

There is more to photography than pointing a camera and clicking the shutter, and creating a really good photograph requires knowledge and skill. The picture should be composed carefully – just like a painting – and should look well balanced and have a central point of interest, or focal point. It is also important to get the lighting right, to avoid making the subject appear too dark or too pale on the print.

◀ *David Hockney is an artist who works with many different materials. This portrait of his mother is a photographic collage. He has taken several photographs of his mother and the room she is sitting in and then arranged them to make one large picture. This way he can include all kinds of details which he could not fit in the frame of one photograph. The shoes in the front are one example. Whose are they? What does the picture tell you about Hockney's mother's life and interests?*
[My Mother, Los Angeles 1982, *David Hockney*]

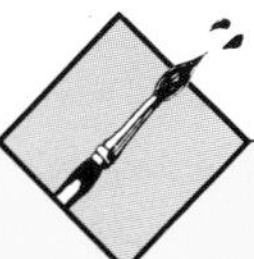

## Make a photo collage

Look at the photographic collage by David Hockney. You can make a simple version yourself, like the example here.

**What you need**

- simple camera (a Polaroid is easiest)
- roll of color or black and white print film
- some friends
- paper
- glue
- black felt-tip pen

**What you do**

1. Get your friends to do something together, such as play a game of cards or look at a book together. Something not too active is best.
2. As they are playing, or reading, take lots of photographs, some of one person, some of the other, some close-ups of the cards or the book, some of your friends' hands. Use a whole roll.
3. If you use Polaroid film, you can start right away. Otherwise, get your film developed.
4. Choose pictures that show your friends wearing different expressions and pictures that show the game at different stages.
5. Arrange them on cardboard, cutting them up so they make a good design and tell a story.

The French painter Paul Gauguin took genre painting one step further. He traveled to the Pacific island of Tahiti to paint the people who lived there. His colorful paintings told the story of life in another country at a time when ordinary people could not travel and see for themselves. By the end of the nineteenth century, religious painting had almost entirely given place to genre painting.

# Stories in print

What is the best story you have ever read? Why did you enjoy reading it? Do you remember the pictures? Did they help you understand the story? Find a favorite book from home or from a library and look at the illustrations.

◄ *This is an illustration from an ancient Persian story, the* Akbarnama. *Adham Khan (wearing the red trousers) has been thrown off the wall as a punishment for murdering Atgah Khan, who can be seen lying at the bottom of the picture. At the very top, another man is scaring birds off the roof of the building. There is a lot of movement and excitement in this illustration. Think how you would divide the stories into separate pictures and put them in order to make a modern comic book story.*

▶ *In the book* Alice's Adventures in Wonderland, *Alice falls down a rabbit hole and meets all sorts of weird and wonderful creatures, most of whom talk a lot of nonsense. In this scene, she stumbles on The Mad Hatter's Tea Party, where there are many places set but only three guests, and not much to eat. Notice how the artist has used only a few pale watercolors. Children's illustrators today tend to use much brighter colors. Looking at this picture, how would you describe Alice's character?* [The Mad Hatter's Tea Party, *from* Alice's Adventures in Wonderland, *by Lewis Carroll, illustrated by Arthur Rackham*]

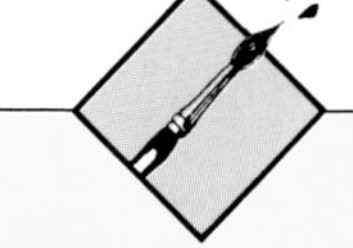

### Write and illustrate a children's book

Do you remember the picture books you had when you were young? Try writing and illustrating one yourself, using a blank exercise book. Give your book a title, cover it, and draw a special illustration for the cover.

Some story books do not have any pictures, but most children's books do. In books for very young children, who cannot read, the style of the pictures is just as important as the words.

Pictures in books are called illustrations because they help to illustrate (explain) the words. When illustrating a book, the artist first reads the story and talks to the author so that he or she can imagine what the characters look like. They decide together which are the best parts of the story to illustrate. Often the author describes the characters and the location of the story in great detail, but sometimes these details are left to the artist's imagination.

### Watercolor painting

Although watercolor paint was used in Egyptian and Oriental painting, it was not used much anywhere else until the eighteenth and nineteenth centuries. Watercolor is made by mixing pigment (color) with gum arabic. Gum arabic is a sticky liquid that comes from acacia trees.

Watercolor is sold in small blocks. To use it, the artist puts his or her brush into some water, then strokes it over the block of paint. The brush picks up the color from the paint, which is then transferred onto the paper.

Some paper for watercolor painting has to be specially "stretched." This is done by soaking the paper with water and then taping it tightly (using masking tape) to a board to dry before use.

Watercolor is versatile. You use it to paint fine detail and to cover large areas. To paint a sky, for instance, wet the paper, then add color to the area with large, sweeping brushstrokes. This is called a "wash." For detail, use a small brush. Mix colors on a plate or the lid of the paintbox.

One drawback with watercolor is that it dyes the paper. It is therefore difficult to correct mistakes. If you apply the paint carefully, you can build up layers of color, as each one shows through the layer beneath it.

## *Fame and fortune*

Many illustrators have made their name by being associated with a particular author. Charles Dickens's novels, written in the nineteenth century, had several well-known illustrators. One of the most famous and popular was known as "Phizz."

Arthur Rackham was a Victorian illustrator of children's books. He used a soft watercolor style that is well suited to the fairy stories he illustrated.

The modern artist Quentin Blake illustrates his own stories and also works with several other authors. He is best known for illustrating the stories of Roald Dahl. His pictures capture the spirit of the stories and the characters in them. Like Phizz, Quentin Blake uses caricature. He makes his figures larger than life and emphasizes their peculiarities, just as Dickens and Dahl do in the text.

It is difficult to recall the stories of A. A. Milne without E. H. Shepherd's delicate drawings of Winnie the Pooh and the other characters.

Beatrix Potter illustrated her own work. Her pictures of Peter Rabbit and his friends have delighted generations of children, and nobody who sees Maurice Sendak's pictures for his book *Where the*

▼ *Comic illustrations have to be strong and exciting to make you want to find out what happens. There are usually some words, but sometimes there will be several frames in a row that will only include sound effects. Yet it is quite clear what is happening in the story. Spider-Man is a famous comic character and, along with Batman and Superman, has many fans – not all of them children.*

*Wild Things Are* ever forgets the dream creatures he depicts or the world they inhabit.

## Tools of the trade

Most book illustrators draw a rough sketch in pencil first before filling the drawing in with color. Many artists use watercolor paint because it is good for painting detail (see page 36). Oil paint is too thick for painting the small, complicated pictures that are generally required for books. Some illustrators use pen and ink. A fine nib is good for drawing intricate shapes and patterns.

## Cartoons and comics

The word "cartoon" these days describes several different kinds of illustration. All rely on strong design for their effect. Drawing must be bold, with clear lines. This

## When cartoons were not funny

The original meaning of "cartoon" was a special charcoal sketch for a painting. When the sketch was finished, the artist transferred the design onto canvas or wood by pricking through the paper with a pin along the charcoal lines. The artist would then paint the picture using the pinpricks as a guideline. Often a cartoon is a masterpiece itself. Leonardo da Vinci's cartoon *The Virgin and Child with St. Anne and St. John the Baptist* hangs in the National Gallery in London.

type of art is called graphic art.

Caricatures are funny pictures of political or other well-known figures whose most recognizable features are exaggerated – often by being drawn much larger than normal – to make them look ridiculous. You will see these cartoons in daily newspapers or satirical magazines. Their purpose is to make fun of the person concerned.

Cartoon "jokes" are usually a single picture, with or without speech, that illustrates one funny idea.

Cartoon strips or comic books are stories told in pictures. The only words that are used are speech, sound effects, and the occasional linking sentence. The cartoonist has to make sure that each picture, or frame, continues from the previous

▲ *Quentin Blake, who drew this picture, has captured the messiness of the boy's bedroom perfectly. He has done this by using loose, sketchy lines and smudgy colors. Compare this technique with that of Arthur Rackham on page 35.*

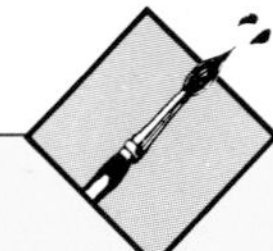

**Profession – cartoonist**

Why not invent your own cartoon character and make up a comic strip? It could be a strange-looking creature from outer space or maybe a comical person with unusual habits. Create a personality for your character and then think of a story to go with it. The story should be simple enough to be told in just three or four pictures. The best comic strips have a joke, or punchline, in the final frame.

To give you some inspiration, here (left) is a strip by Martin Shovel, a professional cartoonist. Notice that the drawing is very simple, and that the character's expressions are very strong and his emotions obvious. You can exaggerate for effect. Snakes do not really have teeth like these, but you can almost feel this one bite!

one, and that the whole story is easy to follow and can be understood instantly.

American artist Roy Lichtenstein liked comics so much that he painted single frames from them onto huge canvases. This type of art, which is based on popular culture, is called Pop art.

## *Famous all over the world*

A cartoonist who is consistently funny and original may become internationally famous. American cartoonist Gary Larson often features animals poking fun at people in his *The Far Side* cartoons. These are syndicated in newspapers and sold all over the world as books and as cards. Charles Addams was popular in the 1950s. His cartoons about the Addams Family were published in the *New Yorker* magazine. The Addamses were unusual. They lived in a huge, spooky old house and looked like vampires. They were miserable most of the time, but this is what was funny about them. The Addams Family cartoon was so successful that a television series and two films have been based on it.

# Moving pictures

What is your idea of a really good film? Do you enjoy sophisticated special effects, like those in Steven Spielberg's films *ET* and *Jurassic Park*? Or perhaps you enjoy animated cartoons? Or films about the martial arts? Or adventure movies? We take films so much for granted these days that it is hard to remember that "moving pictures" have only existed since the beginning of this century, and that television is only about fifty years old.

The invention of film has made a big difference to story-telling. When you read a novel, you use your imagination to conjure up pictures suggested by the words. But in a film or a television program, it is the director who decides how a film should look and uses his or her imagination to create the story in pictures. The director tells the actors and cameramen what to do and oversees all the different stages in making the movie or program.

## *Early days*

Moving pictures were developed by great inventors such as Thomas Edison and Auguste and Louis Lumière. They discovered that if you show a series of different images very fast, one after the other, the eye sees them as a moving object. The camera captures a moving object in a series of still pictures (called

▶ *Charlie Chaplin, seen here in the film* Modern Times, *was a very popular silent movie star. Most people remember him in the role of his most famous character: a down-trodden little man with baggy trousers, a moustache, bowler hat, and cane. In this film, he is working in a factory where the monotony of the work has driven him mad. He is spraying oil at one of his fellow workers. Look at how Charlie is standing, and the expression on the big man's face. In silent films, because there was no speech, movements were exaggerated so that the audience understood exactly what was happening. Actors these days act more naturally.*

Making a film is a little like painting a picture. Actors, props, scenery – all have to be arranged in a way that is attractive and effective.

Next time you watch a film, pretend you are the director. Think how you would tell the actors how to move and what facial expressions they should make. Decide what to say to the cameraman: "Zoom in on that monster, I want to see it close up." Next time you read a novel, think how you would turn it into a film. How could you reduce a full-length story into a ninety-minute film?

frames) onto film. This film is then passed in front of a light and enlarged (a process called projection) onto a screen.

Although they were exciting for their audiences, the earliest movies were much less sophisticated than modern films. They were in black-and-white, not color, and had no sound. A pianist would sit near the front of the theater and play appropriate music for the funny bits, car chases, or romantic scenes. This was a surprisingly effective way of creating atmosphere, and the audience loved it. Between scenes, a card with a caption would flash up on the screen to explain the action to the audience. Special effects were very crude.

Silent film actors had a difficult job. To express their feelings they had to exaggerate their facial expressions and gestures so that there could be no mistake about what was going on.

Some of the best early films were comedies. Charlie Chaplin, Buster Keaton, and Laurel and Hardy were very popular and very funny. Charlie Chaplin's famous character, the Little Tramp, won the hearts of his audience with his bowler hat, walking stick, and bowed legs. His comic, slapstick adventures were often tinged with sadness and sometimes made a moral or political point.

## *Color and sound*

Early color films were extremely crude. An artist had to paint each frame of a black-and-white film by hand. Technicolor, invented in 1915, heralded a new era in filmmaking. Since then, colour films have become the norm.

The next great step forward was the "talkie," film with speech, music and sound effects. The first one, *The Jazz Singer*, was made in 1927.

▼ Robocop *is an action movie that contains a great many special effects. The main character, Robocop, is a policeman who is badly injured, then reconstructed by science to become part-man, part-robot. The construction of his body involved much technical know-how. Not only did he have to look part-machine, but he had to be able to do things that only machines can normally do. A special effects person has to be very skilled in the use of new technology.*

▶ *Although the film* My Left Foot *has no special effects and was made on a small budget, it was very successful and moving. It tells the story of a real person, Christy Brown, who had cerebral palsy, a condition involving weakened muscular power and coordination caused by brain injury, usually at or before birth. Daniel Day-Lewis, the actor who played Christy Brown in the film, won an Oscar for his performance.*

## *Special effects*

Cinema audiences have come to expect films with amazing special effects, many of which can now be designed by computer. Such films depict unknown worlds as if they were real. You can take a trip into space (*Star Wars* and *Alien*), the future (*Back to the Future*), or the prehistoric world of dinosaurs (*Jurassic Park*). Creating these special effects is very expensive, and most films cost millions of dollars to make.

But special effects are not everything. Some of the best movies are made on a small budget. Films such as *Dr. Zhivago, Jean de Florette*, or *My Left Foot*, for example, rely on

◀ *The film* Who Framed Roger Rabbit? *cleverly combined conventional filmmaking techniques with animation. The real characters were filmed first, then the cartoon characters were drawn, and finally the two were combined. This technique provided the filmmakers with all kinds of possibilities. Cartoon characters can fly around, change shape, and do other incredible things that real actors cannot do. But imagine how difficult it is for the real actors to talk to characters that are not actually on the set!*

fine acting, atmospheric camera work, and good stories to attract audiences.

## *Cartoons on the move*

Animated films, or cartoons, do not use real actors or scenery. Animated characters can do anything. Tom and Jerry, the famous cat and mouse partnership, are flattened, cut in two, shrunk, and stretched in the course of a short film, but they always bounce back unharmed.

The most famous animator was Walt Disney.

### Animation

Cartoon characters move around freely, just like real people. What we cannot see is that their movements are made up of many pictures (frames), filmed one at at time and then speeded up; this is called stop-action photography.

A photograph is taken of one frame, then the picture is redrawn or the model moved, only a tiny bit, and another shot is taken. The process is repeated until the film is finished. In most cartoons, the characters are painted on overlays (called cels) and placed on a painted background. Only the moving parts are redrawn.

The movement you see is an illusion produced by the rapid succession of frames. Your eye still carries an image of the previous frame as the next comes into view, and the merging of the two makes you see movement.

There could be as many as sixty different drawings in five seconds of animation. These days, animators use computer graphics to speed things up, but in Walt Disney's day, every cel was drawn by hand.

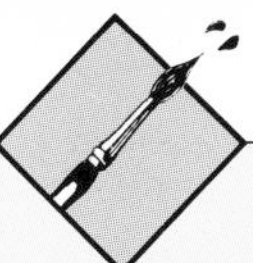

## Flip it

You can create the effect of animation with a single sheet of paper, divided into separate "frames."

**What you need**

- large sheet of white paper
- ruler
- pencil and eraser
- fine-nibbed pen

**What you do**

1. Divide your piece of paper into squares of the same size.
2. In the first square draw a simple picture – a stick person and a ball is an idea to start with. In the other squares draw the same picture but move your character and the ball (or whatever you choose to draw) very slightly so that the action progresses.
3. Cut up the squares carefully. Put the first square on the bottom and work backwards so that the last square is on top. Staple your squares together and flip your book with fingers and thumb to make your film come to life.

His characters, including Mickey Mouse, Donald Duck, and Goofy, were popular with your grandparents and will probably be loved by your children, too. Walt Disney's feature-length films of famous fairy tales still attract large audiences fifty years after they were made.

## *Home movies*

Television was an exciting development in entertainment. In the 1940s and 1950s, cinema became less popular for a while because, suddenly, people could watch moving pictures in their own homes. Television stories come in all shapes and forms – in the news, in plays, in drama series, in films, and in documentaries.

Television documentaries are often about some injustice or terrible situation that most people know little about. It could be a famine in an African country, civil rights here in the United States, or a threat to the environment anywhere in the world. Documentaries can make a difference to how we think about something, and they may even help change the world in some small way.

# About the artists

**ANSDELL, Richard (1815-1885)** This American artist painted dramatic pictures of moments from history. He used bright, luminous colors and strong outlines.

**BENNINCK, Simon (1483-1561)** One of a family of French manuscript painters who are best known for their *Book of Hours*, which shows scenes from the lives of ordinary people.

**BURNE-JONES, Sir Edward (1833-1898)** Burne-Jones was an English painter and designer of stained glass windows and tapestries. His favorite subjects were stories from books, such as Greek myths, Chaucer, and the life of King Arthur.

**DAVID, Jacques Louis (1748-1825)** David was a French painter who started a movement called Neo-Classicism. He looked at sculpture from ancient Greece and Roman (classical art) and used it as a model for his own painting. A supporter of the French Revolution, he became its official artist and had a great influence on art and artists of the time.

**HOCKNEY, David (1937- )** This British artist now lives in California. One of his most famous paintings, *A Bigger Splash*, was painted there. Hockney likes to paint figures, often in bright colors in sunny rooms. He also designs sets for the theater and draws a lot. Since 1980, he has been experimenting with the use of photography, computers, and new technology to create pictures.

**JOHNSON, Eastman J. (1824-1906)** All aspects of American life were painted by this artist, from the lives of African-Americans in the South to those of Native Americans in the North and white farmers in the Midwest.

**KUNIYOSHI, Utagawa (1798-1861)** Kuniyoshi lived and worked in Japan. He produced prints of a variety of subjects including actors, sumo wrestlers, landscapes, Japanese history, and fables.

**LA TOUR, Georges de (1593-1652)** Although he was popular during his lifetime, this French artist was forgotten after his death until 1915. He is most famous for his paintings in which the figures are lit dramatically by one single candle. He painted in warm colors, chiefly red, yellow, and a large range of different browns.

**RACKHAM, Arthur (1867-1939)** Arthur Rackham was an English watercolor artist who is most famous for his book illustrations, especially fairy tales and other children's stories. Titles he illustrated include *The Tempest*, *Rip Van Winkle*, and *Tales of Mystery and Imagination*.

**RIVERA, Diego (1886-1957)** The painter Diego Rivera is most famous for the frescoes he painted on public buildings for the new socialist government of his country, Mexico. He also painted several murals in the U.S., where he lived from 1930-1933. He was married to the artist Frieda Kahlo, whose likeness can be seen in some of his paintings.

**SAHIBDIN, Ustad** Many of the pictures by this seventeenth-century Indian artist illustrate religious books. He used glowing colors and enjoyed painting patterns and decoration.

# Acknowledgements

Michael Holford/British Museum, p.10; Hutchison Library, p.17; Werner Forman Archive/Universitetets Oldsaksamling, Oslo, p.19; ZEFA, p.21; *My Mother, Los Angeles 1982*, © David Hockney, 1982, p.32; Spider-Man: TM & © 1993 Marvel Entertainment Group, Inc. All Rights Reserved, p.37; © Quentin Blake/ Random House Children's Books, p.39; The Kobal Collection, pp.41, 42, 43 (Granada/ Miramax, 1989), 44.

All other pictures are from the Bridgeman Art Library, courtesy of the following organizations: Musée de la Tapisserie, Bayeux, with special authorization of the city of Bayeux, p.4; Giraudon/Musées Royaux des Beaux-Arts de Belgique, Brussels/Giraudon, p.6; Forbes Magazine Collection, New York, p.7; Sean Sprague/Mexicolore, p.8; Birmingham City Museums and Art Gallery, p.13; Maidstone Museum and Art Gallery, Kent, p.14; the Board of Trustees of the Victoria and Albert Museum, London, pp.15 and *cover*, 22, 34; British Museum, London, p.16; Musée des Beaux-Arts, Rennes, p.24; British Library, London, pp.26, 27, 29, 35; Valley of the Nobles, Thebes/Giraudon, p.28; New York Historical Society, p.31.

The photographs on p. 33 are by Zul Mukhida. The illustration on p.18 is by Celia Chester; the cartoon on p. 38 is by Martin Shovel; all other illustrations are by Lis Watkins.

# Index

Addams, Charles 39
Amazons 10
American art and artists 7, 32, 46
animation 44
Ansdell, Richard 7, 46
Arthur, King 13, 14

Bayeux Tapestry 4, 5
beasts 16-21
Benninck, Simon 29, 46
Berlin wall 9
Bible, the 22
Blake, Quentin 36, 39
book illustration 14, 34-39
books of hours 29
Buddhist art 26, 27
Burne-Jones, Sir Edward 13, 14

calligraphy 24
Caravaggio Michelangelo 25
caricatures 38
cartoons 37, 38, 39, 44
carvings 17, 19, 20, 21
Cassatt, Mary 32
Chagall, Marc 7
Chaplin, Charlie 40
Chardin, Jean Baptiste Siméon 31
Chinese art 17-19
Christian art 22, 24
comics 38-9
computer graphics 44

David, Jacques Louis 6, 46
de Hooch, Pieter 30
degenerate art and artists 7
Degas, Edgar 15, 31
Disney, Walt 44-5
Dix, Otto 6
dragons 17-20
Dutch art and artists 15, 30-31

Egyptian tomb paintings 28-9

films and filmmaking 40-41
French art and artists 15, 31, 33
frescoes 8, 9

Gauguin, Paul 33
genre paintings 28-33
Giotto di Bondone 25
Greek art and sculpture 10-12, 16
Greek gods and heroes 10-12, 20
Greek myths 10-12, 16

hieroglyphs 28
Hinduism 27
Hockney, David 32, 46
Hokusai, Katsushika 14, 15
Holy Grail 13
Homer, Winslow 32

illuminated manuscripts 30
Islamic art 24, 25
Italian Renaissance 8, 25

Japanese art and artists 14, 15
Johnson, Eastman J. 31, 46

Koran, the 22
Kuniyoshi, Utagawa 14, 15

La Tour, Georges de 24, 25, 46
Larson, Gary 39
legends 10, 12-15, 16-21
Leighton, Lord 13
Lichtenstein, Roy 39

*Mahabharata*, the 22, 27
Mantegna, Andrea 15
Marat, Jean-Paul 6, 46
marginalia 30
Masaccio 25
masks 20, 21
Middle Ages 4, 17, 25, 29
*Modern Times* 40
Morisot, Berthe 31
Mount Olympus 11
murals 8, 9
*My Left Foot* 42
myths 10-15, 16-21

narrative paintings 7
Nazi Germany 6

oil paint 37

Persian art and artists 14, 34
"Phizz" 36
photographic collage 32, 33
photography 5, 32, 33
posters 7
Potter, Beatrix 36
primitive art 20
propaganda 6

Rackham, Arthur 35, 39, 46
religious paintings 22-27, 33
Rivera, Diego 8, 46
*Robocop* 42

Sahibdin, Ustad 27, 46
Sendak, Maurice 36
Shepherd, E.H. 36
silent films 40, 42
Soviet Union 6, 7
special effects 42, 43
Spider-Man 37
Spielberg, Steven 40
stained glass 22, 23
stonemasons 17
stop-action photography 44

tapestries 5
television, 40, 45
totem poles 20-21

Van Gogh, Vincent 15
Vermeer, Jan 30
Victorian art and artists 13-14, 32
Vikings and their art 19-20

wall hangings 5
wall paintings 7, 8, 28, 29
war artists 5, 6
watercolor paint 37
Watts, George 13
*Who Framed Roger Rabbit?* 44
Wilkie, Sir David 32
woodblock printing 14
woodcarvers 17